Twenty to Make

Pompom
Christmas

Alistair
Macdonald

earch Press

First published in 2015

Search Press Limited
Wellwood, North Farm Road,
Tunbridge Wells, Kent TN2 3DR

Print ISBN: 978-1-78221-346-8
EPUB ISBN: 978-1-78126-392-1

Suppliers
If you have difficulty in obtaining any of the
materials and equipment mentioned in this book,
then please visit the Search Press website for
details of suppliers: www.searchpress.com

Printed in Poland

Dedication
For our 'wee' pompom, TSM.

Contents

Introduction

Pompoms were originally used to decorate naval uniforms, to rank clergymen and to embellish the clothes of people celebrating in national dress. The word itself derives from the French word *pompon*. Today pompoms are a mainstay for many a crafter, but this book seeks to take them to another level altogether!

Christmas is very special for many people and it is great to create your own decorations to put up around the house, or to give as a gift to a loved one. There is nothing better than the satisfaction you get from making something yourself – something to be proud of.

This book covers a whole range of Christmas decorations and plenty of familiar Christmas characters too. Look inside to meet some of them: Rudolph with his red nose, Santa and Mrs Claus, a 'frosty' snowman and my personal favourite, a mischievous Scottie dog – well, I am Scottish!

All of the designs are easy to follow and come with step-by-step instructions, using the traditional cardboard ring method of making pompoms, or the more modern plastic pompom makers that clip together. 'Pompom-ing' really is easy and I hope the projects in this book spur you on to incorporate this popular craft into your own Christmas.

Now, pick up your yarn, makers at the ready – let's continue this pompom revolution!

Making pompoms the traditional way

1 Cut out two identical cardboard discs to the diameter of the intended pompom. Mark out a smaller circle in the centre of each disc. This will form a hole to allow yarn to be passed through. As a rule of thumb, this circle should be half the diameter of the outer circle. Cut the inner circles out.

2 Hold the two cardboard discs together and start to wind your chosen yarn round the rings. Cover the ring entirely until the hole in the centre has almost disappeared.

3 With fabric scissors, cut through the yarn between the cardboard discs round the outer edge. Cut round the entire circumference, releasing all of the yarn and revealing the cardboard discs.

4 Tie a spare piece of yarn between the discs to secure the middle of the pompom.

5 Once knotted securely, tear the cardboard to release the pompom.

6 Finish by trimming the pompom into a neat ball.

Making pompoms with a plastic maker

1 Wind the yarn round one half of the pompom maker.

2 Continue winding until you have created a thick layer, then start winding yarn round the other half.

3 When finished, close the pompom maker and cut through all the yarn.

4 Wind a length of yarn two or three times round the middle of the pompom maker. Pull tight and knot securely.

5 Release the pompom from the pompom maker and trim into a neat ball.

Tools and templates
For all projects in this book you will need fabric scissors and thread snips. Many of the projects also require a long, large-eyed sewing needle in order to thread ribbon through pompoms and attach pompoms to each other. Other tools required are listed on the project pages.

Some of the projects require templates. All templates are reproduced at actual size, so all you need to do is simply trace or photocopy them – easy!

Pompom makers and yarn
I have used the following sizes of pompom makers in this book:

25mm (1in), 35mm (1³/₈in), 45mm (1¾in), 65mm (2⁵/₈in), 85mm (3³/₈in) and 115mm (4½in).

I have used mostly inexpensive acrylic yarn, but remember that many of the projects require only small amounts, which you may already have in your yarn stash.

Rocky Robin

Materials:

1 x 100g ball each of brown-flecked, light beige and burnt orange yarn

Small amounts of orange and brown yarn

5 x 30cm (11¾in) chenille sticks

2 x black mounted sew-on gemstones

Black sewing thread

Tools:

Size 65mm (2⅝in) and 45mm (1¾in) pompom makers

Small pliers

Long, large-eyed sewing needle

Regular sewing needle

Instructions:

1 Start by making Rocky's head and body. Open half of one of the pompom makers and wind on some burnt orange yarn. Fill one third of this half (decreasing to nothing as you meet the opposite side). Fill the remaining space with the light beige yarn. Fill the other half of the maker in the same way but use half as much orange yarn and swap the light beige for the brown-flecked yarn. Repeat the process with the other size pompom maker using the same colours. Trim each pompom into a neat ball. Attach the head to the body, sewing through both pompoms with yarn (see the photograph for positioning).

2 The legs, wings and beak are each made using the following method. One full chenille stick is required for the legs, one for each of the wings, plus a small piece for the beak. For the legs, wind a mixture of brown and orange yarn over a chenille stick to cover it completely. Then bend each end into a foot-like shape (see inset photograph opposite). Once you are happy with the shape created, close each foot by sewing the loose end to the rear of the foot, securing with a stitch. Bring the feet together to locate the middle of the chenille stick. Bend the middle section to form a

shelf-like structure, running parallel with the base of the feet. This will give the body of the robin something to sit on. Position the body on to the feet and secure into position, sewing through the pompom body with yarn.

3 For the wings, find the centre of a chenille stick and wind the brown yarn round until you create a little mound of yarn in the centre. Bring the stick's ends together and continue to wind the yarn, encasing the sticks. Build the yarn up until you have the desired shape. Secure the yarn by sewing down at the smallest end. The beak is made using the same method as the wings, but with a smaller piece of chenille stick, about 4cm (1½in) long.

4 Hold the wings to the body to check the size. You can reduce the length of the wings by bending the smaller ends over if required. Wind some extra yarn round to hide the join and secure with another stitch. Once a pleasing shape has been achieved, sew the pieces directly onto the robin's body. Bend the wings into position.

5 To bring Rocky to life, sew the beak into position with yarn and the gemstone eyes with black sewing thread.

Pompom Bauble

Materials:

Small amounts of red, white and green yarn

Scrap of red satin ribbon, 3mm (1/8in) wide

Glass bauble of the desired size (I used one with a 90mm (3½in) diameter)

Tools:

Size 25mm (1in) pompom maker

Egg cup

Instructions:

1 Remove the bauble top and place to one side. Sit the glass bauble on the egg cup to stop it from rolling away.

2 Make up two pompoms in each colour of yarn, so you have six in total. Trim each pompom into a neat ball.

3 Once you are happy that all six pompoms are of equal size and shaped carefully, insert them into the glass bauble. Use the top of a pen rather than your finger – glass baubles can break easily. A little pressure should be enough to push them through the neck of the bauble. Never use a metal instrument, as this may crack the glass.

4 To finish, carefully replace the bauble top and add some red ribbon to allow it to hang. Trim to the desired length and secure with a knot.

Try out different ideas for your bauble, such as using tinsel yarn. You could add more pompoms, or even stick rhinestones to them.

Garland

Materials:

Small amounts of red, white and green yarn
(or 1 x 100g ball each of red, white and green
yarn if you are making a long garland)

Red double-sided ribbon, 3mm (¹/₈ in) wide (this
should measure the desired finished length
of the garland)

Tools:

Size 35mm (1³/₈ in) pompom maker

Long, large-eyed sewing needle

Instructions:

1 Once you have decided on the desired
finished length of the garland, you need
to work out how many pompoms will be
required. The simplest way to do this is to
divide the length of the garland by the spacing
measurement from one pompom to the next.
For example, if you wish to make a garland
2m (2¼yd) long with the distance between each
pompom centre about 10cm (4in), you need
to divide 200cm (78¾in) by 10cm (4in), which
equates to 20 pompoms. Bear in mind that the
longer you make your garland, the more yarn
you will need.

2 Divide the number of pompoms you are
going to make by the number of yarn colours
you are using. In this case, we are using three
colours of yarn. Always round the number up
(better to have more pompoms than you need).
Make up the required number of pompoms per
colour, then trim each pompom into a neat ball
using fabric scissors and place to one side.

3 Thread the red ribbon into the long,
large-eyed sewing needle and start adding
the pompoms to it. Do this gently to avoid
pulling yarn out of the pompoms. Thread the
pompoms on to the ribbon, alternating the
colours and spacing them evenly. Continue
until the length of ribbon is full.

4 Tie a small loop at each end of the garland
to allow it to hang.

*To make your garland
different, you could try using
a variety of pompom sizes.*

Christmas Tree

Materials:

2 x 100g balls of green yarn in different shades
(I have used a dark bottle green and a lighter
racing green)

Small amount of yellow yarn

Small amounts of red and white/cream chunky yarn

Piece of cardboard (parcel box cardboard is best)

Scrap of green felt

2m (79in) length of green ribbon, 20mm (¾in) wide

Dry-cleaner's metal coat hanger

Tools:

Paper scissors

Size 115mm (4½in), 85mm (3³⁄₈in),
65mm (2⁵⁄₈in) and 35mm (1³⁄₈in)
pompom makers

Glue gun

Heavy duty wire cutters

Pliers

Compasses and pencil

Long, large-eyed sewing needle

Instructions:

1 The tree body is made up of five pompoms. Make two pompoms each using the 115mm (4½in) and 85mm (3³⁄₈in) makers. Make one pompom using the 65mm (2⁵⁄₈in) maker. When making the pompoms, wind the dark green and the lighter green yarn onto the makers at the same time. This will mix the colours evenly. When the pompoms are made, set them to one side – do not trim at this stage. You need to keep a ragged-looking shape as this will help create a realistic tree effect.

2 Set the compasses to 5cm (2in). Mark out four circles on the cardboard and cut them out using paper scissors. These will be used to make a base for the tree to sit on. Now take a dry-cleaner's coat hanger and carefully cut the longest part of the frame free using wire cutters. Discard the rest of the hanger. Using a set of pliers, bend over a 25mm (1in) length away from one of the tips. This will create an L-shaped piece of wire. To build the stand, glue three of the card circles one on top of the other. Find the centre of the fourth cardboard circle and pierce the wire through the centre. Glue this final circle to the other three, trapping the short length of the wire between the layers.

3 Disguise the cardboard rim by wrapping green ribbon round the base. Continue until the circumference is covered. Glue to secure. Wrap a second piece of ribbon round the base and tie a bow to secure. Trim the end to decorate. This will become the front of the

tree. Set the compasses to 5.5cm (2¼in) and draw a circle on to some green felt. This is slightly bigger so that it hides the base. Cut out carefully and glue it to the base.

4 Assemble the tree body by threading the pompoms onto the wire. Start with the largest and end with the smallest at the top. Bend the remaining wire over at the top and conceal in the top pompom. You may need to trim the wire before bending. Make sure that all of the longer ragged ends on the pompoms are positioned on either side with the bow in the centre (see the photograph for guidance). Trim down the centre of the tree's body, both back and front, to neaten, but leave the ragged sides untouched.

5 For the star, make five pompoms using the 35mm (1³⁄₈in) maker and the yellow yarn. Trim to form neat balls. Thread the five pompoms together to form a ring using leftover yarn and tie together to secure. Trim off the excess yarn. Before adding the star to the top, tie a length of red and white chunky yarn together and glue to the top of the tree. Twist the yarn along its length so that the colours alternate and coil it round the tree. Continue until you reach the base. Tuck the chunky yarn towards the underside of the tree and glue to secure.

6 Finish by sewing the star on to the top of the tree using some yellow yarn. Position the star to stand up proud. Stand back and admire your work!

Rudolph

Materials:

1 x 100g ball each of two shades of brown yarn
(I have used chocolate brown and mid-fawn)

Small amounts of red yarn and brown yarn

Scrap of brown felt

8 x 30cm (11¾in) chenille sticks

1 x 40cm (15¾in) length of 1cm (³/₈in) width
red ribbon

Small gold bell

2 x black sequins

2 x white highball buttons

Fabric glue

Tools:

Size 115mm (4½in), 85mm (3³/₈in), 65mm (2⁵/₈in),
45mm (1¾in), 35mm (1³/₈in) and 25mm (1in)
pompom makers

Long, large-eyed sewing needle

Instructions:

1 Start by making Rudolph's head and body. These are made in the same way. Open half of the required pompom maker and wind on some of the fawn-coloured yarn. You are aiming to fill one-third of this half, decreasing to nothing as you meet the opposite side. Fill the remaining space with the chocolate brown yarn. Fill the other side in the same way, but this time use only the chocolate brown yarn. Repeat this process until you have completed three of the sizes required: one each of the 115mm (4½in), 85mm (3³/₈in) and 65mm (2⁵/₈in) makers. Remove the pompoms and trim into neat balls. Connect the pompoms, smallest to largest, with the two larger ones making up the body and the smallest one the head. Make the ears in the same way using the 35mm (1³/₈in) maker.

2 Once the body is securely connected to the head, start to trim the surface of the pompoms until they blend together. The joins should fade into the next pompom seamlessly. You want to achieve a cone shape. Trim the bottom of the cone to create a flat base.

3 To make the snout, use the 45mm (1¾in) and 35mm (1³/₈in) makers and some fawn-coloured yarn. Make a further pompom using red yarn and the 25mm (1in) maker. Connect the two fawn pompoms and trim into a cone shape as above. Trim the red pompom into a neat ball and attach to the top of the cone using spare yarn. Now position the snout and attach to the head. With the snout in place, sew the ears to either side of the head. Trim to blend the joins.

4 Each antler requires four full chenille sticks. Start by making a fold in each stick about 2.5cm (1in) down from one of the ends. Wind the yarn at this folded point to create a little mound of yarn in the centre. With the mound complete, fold the chenille stick end parallel to the main body of the stick and continue to wind the yarn, encasing the folded end. Build the yarn up until you have covered the entire chenille stick. Secure the yarn by tying off. Repeat this process until you have completed three for each antler. With the two remaining chenille sticks, use the same process as above but create mounds at both ends.

5 Twist three of the covered chenille sticks together and bend the tips to create an antler shape. Bend the double-ended chenille stick in half and attach it just below the point where the three chenille sticks divide. Bend into position. Repeat this to create the second pair of antlers. Then twist the bases of the antlers together and disguise the join with matching yarn. Bend together into a V-shape and secure in place, using spare yarn and a needle, at the back of Rudolph's neck (see inset photograph opposite).

6 Sew on the eyes and cut out two semicircles for eyelids from scraps of brown felt. Glue them into position, covering half of the eyeball. Glue a black sequin to the centre of each eye. Thread a bell on to some red ribbon and tie it round Rudolph's neck, complete with a bow.

Santa Claus

Materials:

1 x 100g ball each of red and white yarn

Small amounts of red and beige chunky yarn

5 x 30cm (11¾in) chenille sticks

1 x wooden ball, 5cm (2in) in diameter

20cm (7¾in) length of gold craft wire

Small toilet roll inner

Tools:

Paper scissors

Size 85mm (3³⁄₈in) and 25mm (1in) pompom makers

Long, large-eyed sewing needle

Glue gun

Black marker pen

Pink blending pencil

Instructions:

1 Start by making a frame for the hat. Lay three chenille sticks across each other to form a star shape. Twist the sticks together and mould into a cone shape. Cut a 1cm (³⁄₈in) section from the toilet roll inner (keep it as a ring) and attach the chenille stick ends, spacing them evenly round the circumference of the cardboard, by folding them under and round the card. Once secure, bend the cone shape over to make the base for the hat. Cover the entire shape with the chunky red yarn, concealing the card and sticks. Secure the yarn by gluing.

2 To make the rim of the hat, cover two chenille sticks in white yarn. Fold about 7.5cm (3in) of each end of the sticks into the centre so that they meet in the middle and flatten the sticks using your fingers. Then hold both sticks together lengthways and wind more white yarn around to encase them. Continue until you reach a desired thickness. Bend this piece round the base of the red hat and secure by stitching at the rear with spare white yarn.

3 Using the 85mm (3³⁄₈in) pompom maker, make one pompom in red yarn. Using the 25mm (1in) maker, complete a second pompom in white yarn. Trim into neat balls using fabric scissors. Glue the wooden ball on to the top of the red pompom. Draw on the eyes and add some rosy cheeks using the pen and pencil. Glue the white pompom to the end of the hat.

4 The same method is used to construct both the beard and hair. Cut ten lengths of beige chunky yarn approximately 20cm (7¾in) long. Tie the yarn in the centre to combine and

secure. Make a second bunch of yarn in the same way. Glue one bunch onto Santa's face to create a beard. The knot should face towards the wood to conceal it. Spread the yarn across the face, sticking it into position with some glue. Trim the beard into shape, using the photograph for guidance. Glue the second bunch to Santa's head, using the same method, to create the hair. Glue the hat onto the head and trim Santa's hair as desired. Sew a loop of red yarn on to the hat to allow it to hang.

5 The final touch is to construct a pair of spectacles. Take the craft wire and wrap it round a pen twice, about 5cm (2in) away from one of the ends. This will create one of the lenses. Leave a small gap and repeat the process to form the spectacles. Cut the wire 2.5cm (1in) away from each lens and bend inwards. Place the spectacles on to Santa's head and glue into position.

Festive Wreath

Materials:

2 x 100g balls each of five different shades of green yarn

1 x 25cm (9¾in) diameter flat-backed styrofoam ring

Green cotton fabric, torn into strips 2cm (¾in) wide (you will need 3–4 strips depending on the length of the fabric)

Double-sided red satin ribbon, approx. 5cm (2in) wide and 1.5m (59¼in) long

Double-sided green satin ribbon, approx. 1cm (½in) wide and 60cm (23½in) long

Green embroidery thread

Circle of green, red or burgundy felt, 25cm (9¾in) in diameter

Fabric glue

Tools:

Size 85mm (3³/₈in), 65mm (2⁵/₈in) and 45mm (1¾in) pompom makers

Long, large-eyed sewing needle

Tailor's chalk

Instructions:

1 Make up about 50 pompoms across all the sizes and shades of green. Trim into neat balls and place to one side. To speed up the making process, you can double up the yarn and use two balls of wool at the same time. If you wind four strands of yarn at once, you will fill the pompom makers in no time.

2 Place the styrofoam ring on to the felt, flat side down, and mark round it with chalk. Remove the ring and add a 1cm (³/₈in) seam allowance to the inner and outer lines. Cut out the felt using fabric scissors. This will form a backing to the finished wreath and hide the inner workings.

3 Cover the white ring in strips of green cotton. Wrap the pieces round the ring until you have concealed the white. Secure the ends of the strips by hand sewing onto the ring using green embroidery thread.

4 Now comes the fun part! Arrange the pompoms round the ring and work out a rough positioning. Mix all the sizes and colours to create depth and texture. When you are happy

with the overall shape, attach the pompoms to the covered ring using the long, large-eyed sewing needle and green embroidery thread. Do not be afraid to sew directly through the ring itself. Continue until the ring is covered.

5 To finish, make a large bow from the red satin ribbon and tie it round the bottom of the ring. Trim the ends of the ribbon into a fork shape. Sew a loop of green satin ribbon to the rear at the top of the wreath to allow it to hang. Conceal the raw workings at the rear of the wreath by gluing the pre-cut felt to the back. Hang the wreath to your door and be the envy of your neighbours!

A flat-backed styrofoam ring is ideal for hanging against a flat surface, and makes a sturdy base for the pompoms.

Gift Box Earrings

Materials:

Small amount of red yarn

2 x 30cm (11¾in) lengths of green double-sided ribbon, 3mm (⅛in) wide

2 x gold earring posts

2 x fish-hook earring wires

Tools:

Size 35mm (1⅜in) pompom maker

Long-nosed pliers

Instructions:

1 Using the 35mm (1⅜in) pompom maker, make two pompoms in red yarn. Trim to make a flat surface anywhere on one of the pompoms. Do not go too deep to start. With the flat part in eye line, trim another side at a right angle. Turn this new levelled line to your eye line and continue trimming at right angles. Once you have four equal sides, trim the last remaining

sides to form a cube. Trim carefully until you are happy with the size and shape. Repeat this process with the second pompom to produce a second identical cube.

2 Tie some green ribbon round each cube in the same way as you would round a large gift-wrapped present and finish by tying it into a small bow. Take your time with this step as it is rather fiddly.

3 Now thread the earring posts through the centre of each pompom, making sure that the tied bows are off centre and visible. See the photographs for positioning.

4 Use the long-nosed pliers to snip the posts 1cm (⅜in) away from the pompom. Use the ends of the pliers to create a loop at the end of the post and attach the fish hook earring wires. Close the loops to secure. Now it's party time!

These cute pompom earrings can be personalised very easily. Try using gold or silver ribbon, or even sparkly, metallic yarn to emphasise the festive feel!

Christmas Card Pegs

Materials:

Small amounts of of red and white yarn

Red double-sided satin ribbon, 1.5cm (½in) wide, the desired length

Scraps of light and dark green felt

6 x wooden spring-loaded laundry pegs

Craft paper or card

Tools:

Paper scissors

Size 25mm (1in) pompom maker

Glue gun

Pencil and tailor's chalk

Instructions:

1 Start by deciding how long you wish the ribbon that will suspend and display your Christmas cards to be. Tie a knotted loop at either end to allow it to hang and place it to one side.

2 Decide on a number of pegs to make. For each peg, use either red or white yarn to determine the berry type.

3 Either trace or photocopy the holly leaf template below onto some craft paper or card, then cut it out using paper scissors. Use this template and tailor's chalk to mark out as many leaves on the scraps of felt as you require. As a

ratio, I have used three leaves per peg and 2:1 per colour. Cut out all the leaves and place to one side.

4 To complete a berry, make a pompom using either red or white yarn and a 25mm (1in) pompom maker. Make two berries per peg. Trim the pompoms into neat balls and set aside.

5 Assemble each peg by layering three leaves, alternating the colours. Attach the leaves to the peg using the glue gun. At the same time, glue two berries together and then on to the holly leaves. See the photographs for guidance on positioning leaves and berries.

6 Complete this process until you have enough pegs, then hang your cards to dazzle your Christmas guests!

These pretty pegs are quick and easy to make – if the postman brings more cards than you anticipated, just make a few more!

Holly leaf template: actual size

Angel

Materials:

1 x 100g ball of white yarn
Small amount of yellow yarn
Small amount of beige/cream chunky yarn
Wooden ball, 5cm (2in) in diameter
Pre-wired hackle feathers in white

Tools:

Size 85mm (3³/₈in) and 25mm (1in)
    pompom makers
Long, large-eyed sewing needle
Glue gun
Black pen
Pink blending pencil

Instructions:

1 Using the 85mm (3³/₈in) pompom maker, make one pompom in white yarn. Then, using the 25mm (1in) maker, make five pompoms in yellow. Trim into neat balls and place to one side. Glue the wooden ball on to the top of the white pompom. Draw on the eyes, mouth and rosy cheeks using the pen and pencil.

2 To construct the hair, cut ten lengths of beige chunky yarn approximately 20cm (7¾in) long. Tie the yarn in the centre to combine and secure. Glue the bunch of yarn on to the angel's head. The knot should face towards the wood to conceal it. Spread the yarn round the head,

securing it in position with some glue. Trim the hair into shape, using the photographs for guidance.

3 To form the halo, thread the five yellow pompoms together using some spare yellow yarn. Tie the two yarn ends together to secure. Trim off the excess. Lightly glue the halo onto the top of the angel's head.

4 Finish by twisting together a bunch of pre-wired hackle feathers (about five per wing). Part the feathers to create a pair of wings. Sew them to the rear of the pompom body using spare white yarn. Tie to secure.

This charming angel can adorn your Christmas table or mantelpiece – if you attach some yarn to her halo, you could even hang her on your tree.

Christmas Pudding

Materials:

1 x 100g balls each of brown and black yarn

Small amount of red yarn

Piece of white felt, 14 x 14cm (5½ x 5½in)

10 x pieces of green felt, 3 x 8cm (1¼ x 3¼in)

Craft paper

Tools:

Paper scissors

Size 115mm (4½in) and 35mm (1³/₈in)
   pompom makers

Glue gun

Tailor's chalk

Icing template:
actual size

Instructions:

1 To make this delicious Christmas pudding, use a 115mm (4½in) maker to make a pompom in brown and black yarn. Use a ratio of two brown to one of black. Wind the three yarns onto the maker at the same time for a consistent colour spread. Trim the pompom into a neat ball. To make the holly berries, make a further three pompoms in red yarn using a 35mm (1³⁄₈in) maker and set aside.

2 Either trace or photocopy the icing template on this page and the holly leaf template on page 24 onto some craft paper or card, then cut it out using paper scissors. Use tailor's chalk to mark out the icing shape onto white felt and

the holly leaves onto green felt. Cut them out. Glue the icing on to the top of the pompom and secure the dribbles of icing with a tiny bit of glue near the ends.

3 Attach the holly leaves using the same method. Glue all ten leaves to the centre of the icing section, spacing them evenly round the pudding. Glue the three holly berries to the centre as the crowning glory.

4 To add a further bit of character, fold and arch some of the holly leaves up towards the berries and secure with a little glue. This will give some of the leaves a 3D effect.
Bon appetit!

Napkin Ties

Materials:

1 x 100g balls each of red, white and green yarn (this will make enough pompoms for at least eight napkin ties)

Red double-sided satin ribbon 5cm (2in) wide and approx. 60cm (23½in) long per tie

Tools:

Size 45mm (1¾in), 35cm (1³⁄₈in) and 25mm (1in) pompom makers

Glue gun

Pin

Instructions:

1 First, decide on how many guests you are inviting for Christmas lunch, as this will determine how many napkin ties you require.

2 Make up the following pompoms: 1 x 45mm (1¾in) in white yarn, 2 x 35mm (1³⁄₈in) in red yarn and 2 x 25mm (1in) in green yarn. Trim the pompoms into neat balls and set aside.

3 Cut a section of ribbon 60cm (23½in) long and fold in half. Using a pin, mark the centre of the length. Unfold and lay the ribbon flat.

To assemble the pompoms, start by gluing the white pompom to the central marked point. Follow this by adding a red pompom to either side of the white one, then a green pompom to the side of the red pompoms. The pompoms should be symmetrical through the centre of the white pompom – white, red and green (see the photograph below).

4 Cut the ribbon ends in a diagonal fashion to complete the napkin ties.

These festive napkin ties look great with crisp, white table napkins, adding style to your Christmas table.

Party Glass Markers

Materials:

Small amounts of yarn in assorted colours

Double-sided satin ribbons in assorted colours, each approx. 3mm (1/8in) wide and 25cm (9¾in) long

2 x gold bells, 1cm (3/8in) in diameter per marker

Tools:

Size 25mm (1in) pompom maker

Long, large-eyed sewing needle

Instructions:

1 Make up as many pompoms in as many colours as you think you will need. Cut the corresponding number of ribbon lengths.

2 Trim the pompoms into neat balls and thread up a needle with a length of ribbon. Carefully thread the ribbon through the centre of the pompom and remove the ribbon from the needle. Do this gently to avoid pulling yarn out of the pompom.

3 Tie a bell securely on to each end of the ribbon. This will add some festive cheer and stop the pompom coming loose. Repeat the above process until you have made enough glass markers to go round.

You'll never lose track of your glass with these fun party glass markers!

Snowman Gift Topper

Materials:

1 x 100g ball of white yarn

White sewing thread

Twigs from the garden

5 x small, horn-effect buttons (shirt button size)

2 x sequins

Scrap of orange felt

Wrapping paper and ribbon of your choice

Tools:

Size 85mm (3³/₈in), 65mm (2⁵/₈in), 45mm (1¾in)
    and 35mm (1³/₈in) pompom makers

Long, large-eyed sewing needle

Glue gun

Instructions:

1 Using the 85mm (3³/₈in), 65mm (2⁵/₈in) and 45mm (1¾in) pompom makers, make three pompoms, one in each size, in white yarn. Trim each of the three pompoms into neat balls. Join them together using spare white yarn and the long, large-eyed sewing needle. Begin with the largest and graduate to the smallest. Your snowman should be three-tiered.

2 Roll the scrap of orange felt up into a small cone shape and sew together using white sewing thread. This cone will form a nose and should measure about 3cm (1¼in) in length and 1cm (³/₈in) in diameter. Glue the nose to the snowman's face.

3 Glue the sequins in place for the eyes and add the horn buttons vertically down the

snowman's front. Trim the twigs into the desired shape and position them on either side of the body. Glue into position.

4 Make a further three pompoms using white yarn in the following sizes: 2 x 45mm (1¾in) and 1 x 35mm (1³/₈in). These will decorate the surrounding area where the snowman is to sit. Trim into neat balls.

5 Wrap your gift in the paper of your choice and attach some ribbon. Do not tie a bow and keep the ribbon flat over the gift. You can hide the raw edges under the mounted snowman. Arrange the snowman and surrounding snowballs as shown in the photograph opposite. Use a glue gun to stick them down securely. Now for the other 59 presents!

*The beauty of this snowman is
that he will go with any colour or
pattern of wrapping paper that you
choose. Select a matching ribbon
for the perfectly wrapped gift.*

Elf Christmas Stocking

Materials:

1 x 100g ball of white yarn

1 x piece of red cotton fabric approx. 1m (39½in) long and 112cm (44in) wide

Green double-sided satin ribbon, 5cm (2in) wide and approx. 1m (39½in) long

Green double-sided satin ribbon, 1.5cm (½in) wide and approx. 60cm (23½in) long

Toy stuffing

Sheet of A3 paper

Sewing thread

Tools:

Paper scissors

Size 65mm ($2^5/_8$in), 45mm (1¾in) and 35mm ($1^3/_8$in) pompom makers

Glue gun

Pencil and tailor's chalk

Sewing machine

Pins

Instructions:

1 First, make a template for the elf stocking. On a sheet of A3 paper (297 x 420mm/11.7 x 16.5in), use a pencil to draw a freehand stocking shape with a curled pointy toe. You should fill as much of the space on the paper as you can. Cut round your lines. Do not add any seam allowance as there will be enough to take from this created pattern.

2 Use the template to mark out two stockings with tailor's chalk on to the red cotton fabric. Cut this out with the fabric doubled. One pair will form the outer stocking and the other a lining. Cut off the toe section from the lining pieces to aid turning through and stuffing.

3 Separate the two stocking fronts. With the right side facing you and the pointed toe to your left, lay out some wide green ribbon on to the red fabric. Space it evenly and in a diagonal direction and pin to secure (see the photograph opposite for guidance). I have used three stripes; however, if your ribbon is thinner you could add additional stripes. Top stitch these pieces to the stocking using a sewing machine and a medium stitch length. Continue until all the sections have been completed. Remove the pins.

4 Separately pin the stocking outers and linings together with right sides facing. Machine stitch 1cm ($^3/_8$in) away from the raw

edges, leaving the stocking open at the top. Repeat for the lining, but this time leave the stocking top and toe open. Once completed, bring together the rims of both the outer stocking and the lining. Pin together with right sides facing, taking care to match the side seams. Stitch together using a 1cm ($^3/_8$in) seam allowance. Clip into the curved lines and turn through. Feed the lining back into the stocking and top stitch along the rim 5mm (¼in) from the edge. Stuff the toe with toy stuffing.

5 Along the rim find the centre back seam and add the 1.5cm (½in) wide green ribbon, which will act as a tie. To do this, fold the ribbon in half to find the centre and machine sew onto the outer part of the stocking. Trim the ribbon ends diagonally to neaten.

6 With the stocking completed, make up the following pompoms: 2 x 65mm ($2^5/_8$in), 5 x 45mm (1¾in) and 1 x 35mm ($1^3/_8$in). Trim into neat balls. Use a glue gun to attach seven pompoms in a random fashion to the front of the stocking top and the smallest pompom to the pointed toe (see the photograph for guidance). Then fill with goodies!

Gingerbread Man

Materials:

1 x 100g ball of gingerbread-coloured yarn

Yellow 3D fabric paint

White ribbon bow

2 x black sequins

3 x green buttons

Scrap of red embroidery thread

Fabric glue

Tools:

Size 65mm (2⅝in), 45mm (1¾in) and 35mm (1⅜in) pompom makers

Long, large-eyed sewing needle

Instructions:

1 Make the following pompoms using gingerbread-coloured yarn: 1 x 65mm (2⅝in), 1 x 45mm (1¾in) and 6 x 35mm (1⅜in). Trim the 65mm (2⅝in) and 45mm (1¾in) pompoms into neat balls. Connect the two together to form the body and head using a needle and some spare yarn. After joining, cut across the pompoms front and back to produce two level surfaces. This is to create a flatter, biscuit shape rather than a domed appearance.

2 Trim two of the 35mm (1⅜in) pompoms into neat balls. These are to form arms. Attach these to the body with a needle and some spare yarn. The remaining four pompoms will form the legs. Join two pompoms together with yarn and tie to secure. This will form a sausage-like shape. Level off one of the shorter ends and trim the other surfaces into a neat leg shape, blending the join. Repeat the process for the second leg.

3 Attach the legs to the body and secure with yarn. With the body as a guide, level the legs and arms in line with the rest of the gingerbread man. This will ensure a flat appearance. Add a loop of yarn through the head to allow it to hang.

4 Now for the fun part! Squeeze the yellow 3D paint round the perimeter in a wiggly line to replicate icing. Use fabric glue to add the sequin eyes, bow and buttons down the chest. Once the paint and glue have dried, give your gingerbread man a smile using some red embroidery thread and a needle. Make as many as you like, but don't eat too many!

Mrs Claus

Materials:

1 x 100g ball of red yarn

Small amount of beige/cream chunky yarn

Scrap of green yarn

2 x red silk squares, 19 x 19cm (7½ x 7½in)

Green cotton square, 17 x 17cm (6¾ x 6¾in)

3 x horn buttons (shirt button size)

Wooden ball, 5cm (2in) in diameter

Small scrap of green felt (optional)

Tools:

Size 85mm (3³⁄₈in) pompom maker

Pins

Glue gun

Long, large-eyed sewing needle

Sewing machine and thread

Compasses and chalk pencil

Black pen and pink blending pencil

Instructions:

1 Set the compasses to 9cm (3½in) and mark out a circle with a diameter of 18cm (7in) on to the red silk. Cut this out with the fabric doubled and pin with right sides facing. Machine stitch using a 1cm (³⁄₈in) seam allowance and a medium stitch length round the circumference of the circle. Find the centre of one of the circles and cut an opening 2.5cm (1in) long with

a pair of fabric scissors. Use this opening to pull the work through to the right side. Thread the green yarn onto the needle and add a running stitch round the circumference about 1.5cm (½in) away from the edge. Pull both ends of yarn, drawing the circle together to form the hat. Once you are happy with the shape, tie the yarn in a bow to secure and set to one side.

2 Make the shawl using the same method as the hat, but this time fold the cotton in half to create a triangle. Make a smaller opening to turn through, making this the underside of the shawl. Add a felt patch to hide if required.

3 Using the black pen and the pink blending pencil, draw the eyes, mouth and cheeks onto the wooden ball. With one continuous length of beige chunky yarn, add some hair to the head. Twist the yarn into loops to form curls and glue into position. Continue until you have covered the head.

4 Use the 85mm (3³⁄₈in) pompom maker to make a pompom using red yarn and trim into a neat ball. This will form the body. To assemble, attach the body to the head with glue. Position the hat, shawl and horn buttons, again affixing with glue.

Snowball with Santa Hat

Materials:

1 x 100g ball of white yarn
Red felt square, 15 x 15cm (6 x 6in)
Red embroidery thread
White sewing thread

Tools:

Size 65mm (2⁵⁄₈in) and 25mm (1in)
  pompom makers
Glue gun
Long, large-eyed sewing needle
Regular sewing needle
Compasses and chalk pencil

Instructions:

1 Set the compasses to 7.5cm (3in), mark out a circle on to the red felt and cut out using fabric scissors. Fold the circle in half and roll into a cone. Once you are happy with the shape, hand stitch the cone closed along the straight edge using a needle and thread. I have used white thread as I want this to be visible to add some charm.

2 Make up one pompom of each size – 65mm (2⁵⁄₈in) and 25mm (1in) – using white yarn. Trim into neat balls.

3 Glue the hat on to the large snowball pompom and glue the small pompom to the tip of the cone. Bend the tip of the hat over slightly and secure into position with glue.

4 Sew a length of red embroidery thread to the top of the hat just below the pompom to allow it to hang.

You can make these sweet little decorations in any size. Why not make several hats using felt of different colours?

Snowflake

Materials:

3 x 100g balls of white yarn

Tools:

Size 85mm (3³/₈in), 65mm (2⁵/₈in), 45mm (1¾in) and 35mm (1³/₈in) pompom makers

Long, large-eyed sewing needle

Instructions:

1 Make up the following pompoms in white yarn: 1 x 85mm (3³/₈in), 5 x 65mm (2⁵/₈in), 5 x 45mm (1¾in) and 5 x 35mm (1³/₈in). Trim into neat balls. To speed up the process, wind all three balls of wool onto the makers at the same time.

2 Measure out 30 x 3m (3¼yd) lengths of white yarn. Tie the lengths together at one end and divide into three groups of 10. Plait the yarn until you reach the ends. Secure with a knot.

3 To assemble, start with the largest pompom and add five of the 65mm (2⁵/₈in) pompoms round the circumference to create a flower-like shape. Now add a row of the plaited braid securing into the centre of each pompom using spare white yarn and a long needle. When you reach the centre of the pompom where you started, you will need to trim the braid. To do this, simply wrap and tie yarn round the point where you intend to cut. Tie a second section of yarn 1cm (³/₈in) away from the first and then cut through the centre of both. This will stop the braid from coming undone.

4 Now add the 45mm (1¾in) pompoms and, as in step 3, a second layer of braid. Finally, add the 35mm (1³/₈in) pompoms to the tips of the previous round of pompoms to finish. Attach a loop of yarn to one of the outer pompoms to allow the snowflake to hang.

This charming, fluffy snowflake is a little fiddly to put together, but it is a really simple project to make, and well worth the effort!

Scottie Dog

Materials:
2 x 100g balls of black yarn

Tartan wired ribbon, 5cm (2in) wide and 60cm (23½in) long

Tools:
Size 115mm (4½in), 85mm (3³/₈in), 65mm (2⁵/₈in), 45mm (1¾in) and 35mm (1³/₈in) pompom makers

Long, large-eyed sewing needle

Instructions:

1 Start by making the following pompoms: 2 x 115mm (4½in), 1 x 85mm (3³/₈in), 1 x 65mm (2⁵/₈in), 4 x 45mm (1¾in) and 2 x 35mm (1³/₈in). Do not trim them at this stage. Attach the two 115mm (4½in) pompoms together using spare yarn and a needle. Make sure you line up the ragged edges of the pompoms. Place one of the ragged edges face down onto a work surface. Trim the top ragged edge to create the backbone of the Scottie dog. Only trim the immediate top and leave the rest of the yarn long, so that it appears fur-like. Set the body to one side.

2 Next, join together the 85mm (3³/₈in) and 65mm (2⁵/₈in) pompoms. These will form the neck and the head. Once they are securely connected, trim their surfaces until they blend together. One pompom should fade seamlessly into the next, with the join invisible. Aim to achieve a cone-like shape, leaving some of the yarn ragged at the top. Attach to the body, securing with yarn.

3 Join together the two 35mm (1³/₈in) pompoms and shape as in step 2. Sew this on to the rear of the dog to form a 'waggy' tail. Trim two 45mm (1¾in) pompoms slightly, then sew them on to the rear of the head at either side to form ears, and the remaining two side by side on the front of the head to become the dog's snout. Trim into the desired shape, leaving these pompoms ragged for authenticity.

4 Tie a length of tartan ribbon round the neck, finishing in a plump bow. Trim the ribbon ends into a forked shape. As the ribbon is wired, you can manipulate the shape as you wish.

Why not make a white and a grey Scottie dog as well to keep this little chap company!

Publisher's Note
You are invited to visit
the author's website:
www.houseofalistair.com

Acknowledgements
I would like to thank the team at
Search Press, including May Corfield for her
editorial support, Ruth Jenkinson for the
beautiful photography, and Marrianne Miall
and Juan Hayward for the lovely design work.
Also, a special thank you to everyone supporting
me by buying a copy of my Christmas book – I
hope you enjoy it!